D1445229

CHRISTMAS *Classics*

FLORISTS' REVIEW

Designer

---◆---

Talmage McLaurin is the publisher at Florists' Review Enterprises, the floral industry's oldest and only independent publishing house. He has been with the company since 1991. His floral career began in a family-owned flower business.

Talmage has been a member of the American Institute of Floral Designers since 1988. He has made seven presentations to the institute at its National Symposiums, and in 2003 he co-chaired the National Symposium, "The Prairie School." In 2008, Talmage received the AIFD Award of Distinguished Service to the Floral Industry.

Talmage's trends column and designs appear regularly in *Florists' Review* magazine. His work is also featured in a number of books, including: *Wedding Flowers: Ideas and Inspirations* (2012), *Flower Styling* (2011), *Sympathy Flowers* (2011), *Flowers for the Table* (2010), *Wedding Bouquets* (2010), *Ribbons and Flowers* (2008), *101 How-To Favorites Volume 2* (2007), *Flower Arranging* (2007), *Winning Bouquet Combinations* (2006), *101 Great Displays* (2005), *Christmas Traditions* (2004), *Weddings 2* (2004), *Design School* (2003), *101 Wedding Bouquets* (2002), *Seasons of Flowers* (2001), *101 How-To Favorites* (2000), *World Floral Artist 2* (1999), *Weddings* (1998), and *Christmas* (1996).

---◆---

Contents

Woodland

◆

Partridge, quail and rabbit stir

And gambol here and there.

Nature breathes a blessing

On the bracing, wintry air.

– Jim Dunlap
from "A Woodland Christmas"

◆

As if gathered on a winter stroll through the woods, the permanent *Eucalyptus*, berries, pine and cedar play well with preserved reindeer moss, pods and curly willow in this topiary, which celebrates nature's imperfect lines and delightfully random forms.

how-to

Construct a topiary "trunk" of curly-willow branches that are cut to a uniform height. Impale a block of plastic foam by pressing it into the tops of the branches. Secure the insertions with pan-melt glue.

Frost-tipped faux kale leaves cover a basic container to start this tabletop
arrangement, which is a potpourri-collection of cones, berries and branches.
Gold cording and a web of gold bullion wire lend some seasonal sparkle.

Wire urns filled with pine cones and other woodsy accents join wooden candleholders that are cleverly topped with giant cones and feather-covered orbs. Crimson highlights of faux berries, *Hydrangeas* and felt complete the classic tableau.

Subdued hues and a gathering of natural elements that appears to have been plucked during a ride through the countryside beautifully adorn this equestrian-themed vase. The rosette formation of inverted pine cones add interest at the design's focal area.

The cool tones of bleached wood in the candleholders and bowl form a perfect harmony with the berried juniper and icy blue candles while warm coppertone mosaic orbs and amber pine cones establish a contrast to the color story. An orb of blush-colored carnations is featured in the driftwood bowl.

RIGHT A ready-made permanent wreath, composed of hard-shell delights, needs only a sash of ribbon to be presented for the holidays. No nutcracker is required.

LEFT This dramatic centerpiece features simple components that are densely arranged in a classic urn. Fresh apples are laid into the center of the composition along with glittered ornaments that provide a reflective quality with their mix of shiny and matte surfaces. A smilax wreath, laid on the edge of the urn, creates a "well" for the apples and ornaments.

Tied together to form a single centerpiece and filled with a tasteful assortment of fresh red-twig dogwood, velvet-apple branches, lotus pods, pine cones and tallow berries, this trio of baskets takes a back-to-basics approach to the holiday centerpiece.

Permanent and dried materials are arranged into a fragrant
wreath ready-made of fresh greens. Contributing a bit of sparkle
appropriate to the holidays, a few of the elements, including a pair
of eggs, are gilded, nested and tucked into the composition.

Showcasing a cherished ornament with woodland charm, this captivating topiary offers a sturdy yet stylishly simple holiday decorative. Featuring sculptural twigs with a built-in nest and clusters of berries, the design utilizes the humble beauty of nature's materials to contrast a radiant glass orb.

how-to

In a cube container filled with plastic foam and topped with moss, arrange branches to form a tripod on which the nest can be attached. Secure the ornament inside the nest with floral clay.

RIGHT Fragrant, fresh evergreens combined with the elements of a crisp woodland forest form this nature-inspired composition that is upgraded for a home setting with a trio of votive candles in thick glass holders. Wooden eggs inside the nest continue the theme that is established by the rustic rectangular wooden tray.

LEFT Inexpensive glass domes feature a nest-filled still life with unfinished wood bases that are "stained" with a dusting of spray paint so their hue harmonizes with the other wooden accessories.

how-to

Attach a wired wood pick to each pine cone by weaving the wire around the base of the cone, between the scales; twisting it tightly; and wrapping it around the pick.

Wintergreen

◆

A Christmas tree! A Christmas tree!

With dark green needled memories

Of childhood dreams and mysteries

Wrapped present-like in front of me.

– David Keig
from "A Christmas tree! A Christmas tree!"

◆

'Eskimo' roses, miniature *Hydrangeas*, button chrysanthemums, *Trachelium* and *Hypericum* berries mix with chocolate-colored pine cones and shimmering satin ribbon for a verdant holiday bouquet.

LEFT With swirling patterns and a few nods to nature, this contemporary vignette is a show-stopper. A textural planter serves as a sleek tree "trunk" for the collection, which features permanent *Echeverias*, glittered holly, sequin ornaments and black accents to enrich the modern edge.

Nature presents her gifts of the season in this organic grouping, which will pair exquisitely with wood and woodtones as well as items that appear to have been exposed to the elements. Tiny golden baubles add a bit of glam to 'Green Trick' *Dianthuses* and fragrant white pine while an egg-filled nest, in a moss-covered basket, is nature's counterpoint to the shiny sprays.

A bevy of birds flocks in and around this fresh tree, which is in a grower's pot concealed by a ceramic urn. Displayed with the birds, collections of vintage-inspired ornaments, in mercury and clear glass, bedeck the diminutive fir.

Earthy organic elements, like permanent *Eucalyptus*, moss orbs and reindeer moss, cast in a range of greens and winter whites, receive an industrial edge in chrome-colored containers and with platinum-hued accents. Manicured orbs and spheres lend to the seasonal formality.

Dip tufts of reindeer moss into pan-melt glue, and press them onto a plastic-foam cone that is secured into a planter base. The moss cone can be left plain or topped with another glittering cone for added flair.

how-to

Insert mechanical candles into a foam ring at evenly spaced intervals. Follow with insertions of juniper berries, thistles and spray chrysanthemums.

This candle wreath, outfitted with mechanical candles that are loaded with wax inserts for a natural flame, features the detailed textures of juniper berries, globe thistles (*Echinops*) and 'Kermit' spray chrysanthemums, creating an alternative color contrast for green by combining it with gray-blue botanicals.

This holiday collection features an unusual combination of dried tallow berries, *Hypericum*, *Hydrangeas* and green spray chrysanthemums forming the orb accessory. Mercury-glass ornaments pair with green apples to form the arrangement's focal area.

Coil aluminum wire tightly around the stem of the urn, then continue coiling in a looser fashion upward. Pinch the end of the wire over the lip of the urn to secure.

Adding flair to a clear glass urn of 'Super Green' roses, ivy and *Hypericum*, decorative wire creates a distinctive coil around the urn's stem and continues encircling the transparent receptacle in a looser coil. In addition, small pieces of wire are shaped into clever "faux" leaves for fresh 'Granny Smith' apples.

how-to

Bend aluminum wire into an artful wavy pattern, and wrap it around the candle, beginning at the bottom.

RIGHT A squiggly band of apple-green aluminum wire is an arty embellishment to a matching-hued pillar candle. Natural collars of buttonbush (*Berzelia*) and *Hypericum* compose a simple candle-ring-style arrangement and expand the monochromatic palette.

LEFT Offering a modern alternative to a tabletop tree, this arrangement, featuring cut fir, 'Super Green' roses and cushion spray chrysanthemums in a floral-foam filled ceramic container, showcases handmade ornaments created from aluminum wire.

Bend aluminum wire randomly into a long, wavy piece. Then roll the wavy wire into an abstract spherical shape, and smash it to flatten. Leave a portion of wire at the end to attach the "ornament" to the arrangement.

RIGHT An old-fashioned kissing ball receives a modern look with a wrapping of decorative wire and assorted gems and baubles. Green *Hypericum* berries replace the red berries that originally adorned the fresh ready-made orb, creating a monochromatic composition along with the button spray chrysanthemums.

ABOVE Offering two gifts in one, this centerpiece sporting 'Princess' spray roses and fresh pine doubles as a decorator's gift basket since once the roses have faded, five premium ornaments remain to take their place on the tree for years to come.

LEFT Whether the fruit is fresh or faux, creating the neatly stacked column is a simple matter utilizing the time-tested technique of threading fruits onto a dowel. When using permanent apples, as we've done here, a drill is best for boring holes into the foam filling, but with fresh fruits, an ice pick is the recommended tool. Once the fruits are threaded onto the dowel, another hole is required in the topmost apple, into which the candle is nestled.

OPPOSITE PAGE A mix of greens, both fresh and faux, celebrate holiday green in a heavily fruited wreath of pears and apples. The mantel is flanked with two candle-topped urns stuffed with more fruits, pine cones, fragrant winter greens and fresh *Viburnum*.

how-to

Attach a plastic-foam cone into a clay pot using pan-melt glue. Cover the cone with inverted pheasant feathers that are attached with a dot of glue. Add an inverted tussie-mussie holder on top for the tree topper.

LEFT Anything but traditional, this tabletop tree is fashioned entirely from pheasant feathers that are inverted atop a plastic-foam cone. A resin tussie-mussie holder and clay pot are painted to coordinate as the topper and base for this unexpected holiday accent.

BELOW Laid atop an Oriental fishbowl stand, a plastic-foam wreath is the base for this lush centerpiece of woodsy permanent and preserved materials. Permanent *Magnolias* and ornaments join natural pine cones, flat *Protea* flowers, preserved *Hydrangeas* and pheasant feathers.

A collection of mantel arrangements continues the theme of woodland glitz featuring dynamic crossing lines of pheasant feathers joined by glittered *Magnolia* blossoms, cones and gleaming ornaments.

Tantalizing textures and sharp contrast take the reins in this gleaming contemporary setting of pewter, silver and holiday-green accents. A collection of mercury-glass cylinders shares space with candleholders that are painted bright, shiny green. Metallic botanicals and silver jingle bells accent this glittering display.

Candlelight

Sitting under the mistletoe

One last candle burning low,

All the sleepy dancers gone,

Just one candle burning on

— Walter de la Mere
from "Mistletoe "

A poly-film-wrapped floral-foam design bar is a perfect alternative to a container for this hedgelike candle design. The golden texture of five pillar candles, resting atop an arrangement of evergreens, complements the gold-leafed look of the various colors of color-enhanced pods. Perfect for the mantel or as a long centerpiece, the contrast of fresh and gilded materials is enhanced by the glow of the flames.

Position pillar candles evenly atop a floral-foam design bar, and insert wood picks into the foam around the base of each candle to secure it in place.

A dazzling spectrum of colors proclaims the magic of the season while a quartet of carnation varieties adds fresh appeal. The generous application of gold and red keeps the rainbow of color feeling holiday inspired, over which a glittered angel keeps watch.

Tradition

I heard the bells on Christmas Day

Their old, familiar carols play,

And wild and sweet, the words repeat

Of peace on earth, good-will to men!

– Henry Wadsworth Longfellow
from "Christmas Bells"

LEFT A tall red glass vase provides a sophisticated upgrade for this fresh myrtle topiary from its former plastic pot. The base is covered with red metallic jingle bells that beckon a charming bird to join the Christmas setting. The loops of the shoestring-style bow that trails from beneath the myrtle are gently sculpted into heart shapes, providing another simple but noticeable enhancement.

BELOW A plaid ribbon wrap covers the exterior of a wreath ring and echoes the varying hues of long-lasting carnations sprinkled with sparkly baubles while a simple cylinder vase safely encases a candle that seems to be attracting a butterfly to its flame.

OPPOSITE PAGE *Hypericum*, *Eucalyptus* and rose hips lend a very berried texture to this holiday gathering. Fragrant carnations and fir tips join the collection that also features matte and metallic ornaments in a glossy red planter.

how-to

Fill small vases with several blades of lily grass to form an appealing pattern against the clear glass. Insert some with the tips pointing upward and others pointing downward to create an armature to position the flowers.

LEFT Maximum impact is achieved when simple glass vases are filled with lily grass prior to adding a nostalgic mix of roses, holly, *Lysimachia* and *Viburnum* berries.

Sleek black accessories pair with vintage holiday images to showcase the classic red-and-green palette with fresh 'Liberty' and 'White O'Hara' garden-style roses. The holly and the ivy are attractive and lyrical while red *Hypericum* berries are stand-ins for the missing holly berries.

BELOW Transforming a manicured ivy topiary into a holiday show-stopper is fast and easy. Floral adhesive is used to glue on picked ornaments while the redbirds come equipped with handy ornament clips that secure their perch.

ABOVE Tartan antler ornaments decorate the bases of multicolored candlesticks, as plaid ribbons cut into leaf shapes increase the medley of pattern on pattern.

how-to

Spray the backsides of faux poinsettia leaves with adhesive. Press into place onto tartan ribbon or fabric. Trim away excess fabric to achieve the leaf shape.

A set of tin planters is sized to enable a gallant two-tiered arrangement filled with two hues of crimson carnations. Red accents, as well as a cube-shaped vase wrapped with tartan ribbon, continue the traditional flair.

Traditional in their holiday hues, this pair of stylish designs creates a contemporary composite display when placed closely together. The rich velvety colors of scarlet roses, amaryllises and *Astilbe* mixed with vivid verdant fir match those of the gilded holly-patterned containers.

how-to

Drill three evenly spaced holes into the bottom of each pillar candle, and insert wood picks into the holes. Secure each candle atop a foam-filled vase.

how-to

Insert wood picks through a premade wreath into dry foam to anchor the wreath upright atop the foam. Arrange permanent greenery at the base, and tie a bow at the top of the wreath.

Traditional red and green take a twist toward the modern
when the verdant hue is a vivid chartreuse. Playful animal-
striped ribbon and the mix of matte and glossy finishes add
depth and interest.

OPPOSITE PAGE Metallic silver finials and permanent *Ilex*-filled cylinders suggest a romantic winter frost in this setting, which is anchored by a sophisticated wreath of velvety crimson roses.

ABOVE Central in this sterling-colored Revere bowl is a grouping of lush 'Vendela' roses. Surrounded by *Hypericum* and cedar tips, the final touch is perfectly executed as the metallic rose leaves extend a perfect complement to the silvered bowl.

OPPOSITE PAGE Combining classic Christmas colors, this charming design features safely burning mechanical candles secured into a square block of floral foam. Carnations cover the sides of the foam block, and fresh pine needles fill in the top. The most notable aspect of this design is one that is not seen: Rather than sitting in a container, the floral-foam base has a waterproof "seal," created by dipping the bottom side of the foam into the pan-melt glue.

To create a watertight base, place the bottom of a half block of floral foam into enough pan-melt glue to cover the base and about one-half inch up the sides. Let the glue harden, and then float-soak the foam.

LEFT Scarlet red carnations and green *Hypericum* berries, in the holiday's traditional complementary color scheme, beautifully fill a square vase's expansive opening. Normally, filling such an immense space would require significantly more materials, but an organic, handcrafted armature laid atop the vase holds the materials in place and maintains their placement.

how-to

Strip the foliage from 10 to 12 green dogwood branches. Assemble them into an appropriately sized grid, and tie the twigs together with paper-covered binding wire at the points where the twigs intersect.

LEFT A profusion of coiled gold aluminum wire creates an interesting armature for *Gerbera* stems inside a fishbowl-shaped glass vase. The monobotanical display is simple, yet impacting, evoking a jovial mood for holiday festivities. The streamerlike effect of the wire spirals is created by wrapping the wire around a fat marker.

RIGHT Christmas and candles go hand in hand, and this simple design displays true Christmas red in a quartet of tapers. Breaking up the monotony of red, however, are unexpected gold-painted *Galax* leaves that are placed among the roses in lieu of evergreens. The leaves are inconspicuously pinned to the foam with their stems exposed rather than inserted in a normal fashion.

OPPOSITE PAGE A pair of irresistible topiaries, made from mixed berries, wild-looking vines and velvet florals, receives a hint of holiday grandeur when placed atop the gold-striped vessels. The gilded deer repeat the gold striping and accent the scarlet arrangements.

ABOVE Tiny squares of ribbon, cut from bolts in a range of reds, are used to create a visually intriguing tone-on-tone wreath. Silver and pewter disks, from disassembled garlands, add unexpected dimension.

RIGHT Velvet squares, cut from affordable ribbon, in red and cranberry colors, are haphazardly pinned to a plastic-foam cone to create a bright, thoroughly modern presentation.

how-to

Cover a foam cone with squares of ribbon in a random, overlapping fashion, using boutonniere pins to secure the squares to the cone.

Christmas red gets a modern makeover when paired with gleaming silver and polished charcoal and black. The look is sleek and sophisticated but can be tailored to more classic stylings. Sequined ornaments and split pomegranate ornaments look lovely displayed en masse while the flourishing silhouette tree inspires the addition of functional candles.

Cool Yule

◆

And when those blue snowflakes start falling

That's when those blue memories start calling

You'll be doin all right,

with your Christmas of white

But I'll have a blue, blue blue blue Christmas

– Billy Hayes and Jay W. Johnson
from "Blue Christmas"

◆

Coatings of white candle wax add a look of wintry realism to the pine cones nestled within this seasonal arrangement of *Eryngium* and dusty miller, as if the cones were gathered from ground blanketed in newly fallen snow. Teal-blue millimeter balls add holiday appeal while lending shimmery touches to the frosty cool color palette.

how-to

Melt candle wax in a hot-melt glue pan at a low temperature, and carefully drizzle the wax over the nest and pine cones with a spoon.

According to legend, finding a bird's nest within a Christmas tree is considered good luck. This arrangement, featuring a "snow"- covered nest surrounded by wintry juniper and dusty miller, offers a tabletop delight. The nest, which is drizzled with white candle wax, provides a natural focal point that is balanced by pairs of glimmering ornaments and silver pillar candles.

The muted hues of the botanical birch candles and aged containers get a gorgeous punch of color from the sleek and sparkling teal accents, including a bevy of glittering butterflies. The interior-friendly colors give this look winterlong appeal and are a welcome option when red-themed decorations don't comfortably fit the palette.

Scoop out a bit of foam from one end of a foam-centered ornament. Dip one end of the spire into pan-melt glue, and insert it into the cut end of the foam ornament.

LEFT Decorating the door is a hand-assembled swag of permanent greenery bedecked with embroidered leaves and icy blue orbs. A luminous golden ribbon cascades from the swag's center.

BELOW Pearly blue sprays are tucked into a mossy base that surrounds a quartet of fragrant snow-white hyacinths.

OPPOSITE PAGE Ornaments are used to create a series of accent pieces in varying heights that spans the mantel. A cloud of gilded baby's breath is featured near the center. Spray fresh baby's breath with a metallic gold paint for best results. No need to add water to the vase; simply let the stems dry in place.

75

Elegant and ethereal, the glistening silvers and frosty whites of the palette reflect the splendor of a new-fallen snow. Touches of whimsy are added with crystalline butterflies and the jolly-looking silver gnome. The garden urns are transformed to their snowy condition with matte white spray paint.

LEFT Bursting with color and textural interest, this tabletop tree features an eclectic mix of satin corsage leaves, corsage pins, beads and even grapes. A foam cone secured atop a ceramic pot provides the base of the tree, which is completed with swirling wires and a teal-colored ornament topper.

OPPOSITE PAGE Displaying colorful ornaments in a clear glass hurricane makes an instant holiday decoration that is both tasteful and everlasting.

how-to

Cover a plastic-foam cone with sheet moss, and wrap it with wire to hold the moss in place. Attach disassembled grapes to the cone with corsage pins. Add leaves, beads and wire prior to hot-gluing the finial ornament at the top.

Modern Merry

◆

Trim up the tree with Christmas stuff

Like bingle balls and whofoo fluff

Trim up the town with googoo gums

And bizilbigs and wums

– Dr. Seuss
from "How the Grinch Stole Christmas"

◆

how-to

Attach each permanent grape by sticking a boutonniere pin through the grape, then dip the end of the pin into pan-melt glue, and insert it into the foam wreath.

BELOW Add a little fun and whimsy to holiday creations with colorful floral foam. Here, pink foam in two pretty hues is layered into an urn-shaped vase to create a festive striped effect. The delightful mix of flowers includes carnations, *Dahlias*, flame flowers (*Talinum*), snowberries (*Symphoricarpos*) and *Hypericum*.

Slice cylinders of colored floral foam into several thin disks. Layer the disks in alternating colors inside an urn-shaped vase or large cylinder. When arranging flowers, avoid insertions near the perimeter, so stems are not visible around the outer edges of the foam.

OPPOSITE PAGE This berried creation is built on a molded urethane wreath form that is painted black. Faux grapes, cherries, blackberries and other unidentified berries are positioned with black pearl boutonniere pins and hot glue, for a mouth-watering mix while the randomly directed cherry stems create a playful accent.

A fanciful bird — transformed by adding feathers and silver accents — perches on a delightful collection of *Anemones*, *Ranunculi*, *Phlox* and *Eryngiums*. A floating candle emits a warm glow that contrasts the cool tone of the collection while a glass cylinder vase protects the flame from any accidents.

Spray a faux bluebird with silver paint. Secure additional feathers to the bird's tail with bullion wire, and continue wrapping bullion wire around the entire bird. Spray a final coat of metallic silver paint. When dry, attach a wood pick to the bird.

As the "green" movement spreads to the urban jungle, natural organics and urban chic collide. The resulting style, depicted in this environmentally uptown wreath, features contrasting hues of green and purple in artichokes, Osage oranges, *Alliums*, *Tracheliums*, thistles and *Echinops*. A bird and ornaments crafted from discarded newsprint and vintage glass bobbers add a salvaged edge to the mix.

ABOVE Silver accents like this mint julep cup beautifully reflect the delicate femininity of this graceful composition. Faux amaryllis blooms, cockscomb, and *Skimmia* provide a nontraditional holiday palette.

OPPOSITE PAGE Berry colors that extend into the pink, mauve and burgundy color families add yet another color option for custom Christmas decorating. Here a bowl and wreath are created by overlapping gilded *Magnolia* leaves and hot-gluing them onto a wire wreath form and a flared plastic bowl. Rosy pink bell balls and artificial chestnuts fill the bowl to perfection.

ABOVE Modern sophistication and bold graphics fuel this spirited design that begins by painting an inexpensive PVC wreath with raspberry-colored paint. Chartreuse *Cymbidium* orchids and fuchsia *Phalaenopsis* orchids complete the inner rings of the wreath.

OPPOSITE PAGE Peacock feathers have emerged as a popular trend for a variety of occasions. The rich jewel tones of these ornaments extend the theme and add festivity to the holiday season as they are displayed in a trendy glass cloche paired with a bouquet of purple-hued carnations.

Country

---◆---

Over the river and thru the wood,

To grandfather's house we go;

The horse knows the way

To carry the sleigh, thru the white and drifted snow

– Lydia Maria Child
from "Over the River and Through the Woods"

---◆---

OPPOSITE PAGE Classic holiday red merges with the rustic textures of birch and stone for a European-country feel. From the pine cone wreath to the birch-hewn containers and tree to the folk-crafted angel, each element speaks to the vignette's Scandinavian spirit. A collection of faux eggs makes a clever bouquet when accented with a woolly red bow.

Use hot-melt glue to position a thick piece of birch into a container filled with plastic foam. Secure another piece of plastic foam atop the birch log with hot-melt-glue, and arrange permanent blossoms into the foam.

RIGHT A lined boxboard tote in classic Christmas red holds an abundant arrangement of incense cedar, carnations, *Hypericum* and *Thryptomene calycina*. Traditional plaid ribbon wrapped around the handles of the container creates festive flourishes, with imaginative, scroll-like rolled ends, on opposite sides of the arrangement.

how-to

Thread a length of wire-edge ribbon through each opening, and wrap it several times around the handle of the tote. Curl the ends of the ribbon around a pencil.

LEFT Despite its old-fashioned country feel, this Christmas display includes modern flower choices of tulips, carnations and amaryllises, with a mix of fresh and permanent botanicals. Products are grouped for impact, from the charming caroler figurines to the wicker baskets and the materials arranged within them.

OPPOSITE PAGE Jackie berries, which are dried and dyed seed heads, cover this wreath, creating an unusual texture for holiday decoration. Simple yet modern, this thin composition is perfect for narrow spaces, such as between a front door and a storm door on a home.

how-to

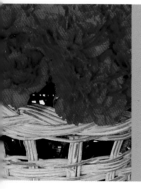

Dip each berry into pan-melt glue, then attach it to a floral-and-craft ring made of particle board, from the inside edge to the outside edge, being sure to cover the entire surface of the ring.

This woodsy setting lends a natural touch to the traditional red and green hues of Christmas. Eye-catching props, such as a rustic lantern filled with ornaments, draw attention and add importance to the items contained within them. Larger versions of the matte-finish ornaments serve as festive focal points in two coordinating arrangements. Sections of each urn are covered with parsley flakes, giving them the look of trimmed hedges.

Wrap painter's tape around the portions of the urn that are to be left bare. Spray adhesive onto the base and top portion of the urn, and sprinkle on parsley flakes to cover the area.

RIGHT Exotic botanicals, arranged as if they were gathered by an artisan for sale at an open-air market, contribute a wealth of worldly hues. This wreath, which is appropriate for fall into the holidays, was built on an affordable PVC evergreen base, and can be punched up with the addition of metallic ornaments or festive ribbons.

LEFT Plaid ribbon squares, in two coordinating patterns, carry visual interest from the mix of fresh incense cedar, fir, *Gerberas* and *Hypericum* and preserved *Hydrangeas* to the base of the elongated mint julep vase. The ribbon squares, which have frayed edges for a modern look, are secured to the vase with hot-glue in an overlapping and alternating-pattern manner to create a decorative vertical strip on the vase.

how-to

Cut ribbon into squares, and strip several threads off each of the squares' four edges to fray them. Hot-glue the squares to the vase.

Created with materials that could have been plucked from the landscape and simply gathered into a bowl, like apples, pine cones, white cypress and cotton, this Colonial-inspired arrangement imbues a sense of rural-American nostalgia. The whimsical elves, in their vintage-looking, holiday-hued garb, are charming accents.

RIGHT A loop of buffalo-plaid ribbon continues the vintage American theme to a ready-made wreath of wooden flowers.

LEFT In a muted color palette reflective of those found in Early American homes, these companion pieces demonstrate a subdued modesty that was typical of the work of New England craftsmen. Their colors and unpretentious styling will appeal to those who yearn for the ease of simpler times. Preserved cedar, preserved juniper, pine cones and *Canella* berries combine for an unassuming holiday statement.

100

A poinsettia-blossom bow, created with classic holiday-hued tartan ribbon, provides distinction beyond a standard bow for this classic Christmas botanical mix of carnations, *Thryptomene calycina* and pine cones. The combination of shades among the materials — from bright and muted reds to white and cream — offer an old-fashioned look, which is further enhanced by the vessel's weathered finish.

how-to

Cut ribbon into several equal lengths, snipping diagonally to create angled edges. Gather the pieces together, crimping them in the centers, and tie another piece of ribbon around the center tightly to secure. Attach to a wired wood pick.

LEFT Using noble fir branches to create a composite tree shape, this delightful decoration could be one of the most charming of conversation pieces. The eclectic presentation features rural charm, with birch branches, pine cones and stick rolls inserted at random. Red spray roses are the flower focus, with their brilliant hue set against the natural colors of woody materials and wintergreens.

OPPOSITE PAGE Textile accents lend a sentimental feeling to this homespun look. Faux apples provide a festive holiday hue in the wreath and throughout, as well as a bit of classic country appeal. The sleek containers, one of which displays a faux boxwood topiary with an ornament collection at its base, ensure a modern vibe.

Confections

---◆---

The children were nestled all snug in their beds,

While visions of sugar-plums

danced in their heads.

And mamma in her 'kerchief, and I in my cap,

Had just settled our brains for a long winter's nap.

– Clement Clarke Moore
from "A Visit from St. Nicholas"

---◆---

Mercury, champagne and ivory are colors that are important to the soft nature of this color palette. When the hues are incorporated, in the form of shimmering baubles, into a peach-colored wreath of fresh 'Ilse' spray roses, the effect is glamorous without ostentation.

Roses, *Lisianthuses* and tulips, gathered into a classic nosegay, harmonize the soft tones of this theme. Faux poinsettia petals add a candlelight-colored glow around the edge of the posy. Exquisite patterned ribbon, tucked between the layers of a vessel crafted for this purpose, repeats the sparkling champagne hues.

Delicate materials and soft, shimmery hues give this display a feminine elegance that has strong appeal. Clear beads and baubles, some with light-reflecting facets, resemble precious gems.

how-to

Insert a taper candle through a hole cut in a small cube of plastic foam. Place a tree topper or other ornament onto the candle, and arrange permanent flowers into the plastic foam.

Vintage wares paired with collected oddities, both old and new, distinguish this nostalgic and quaint wreath. The PVC wreath base is lightly sprayed with an almond-colored paint while antique doilies and preserved roses are colored with coral tones to blend with the candied colors of this palette.

This classic setting, featuring sugar-dusted fruits of the season, offers simply stated old-world elegance. Sugared fruit and foliage decorate a wreath, fill a centerpiece and cleverly occupy the space in an antiqued cream wire birdcage.

President: Frances Dudley, AAF

Publisher: Talmage McLaurin, AIFD

Floral Designer: Talmage McLaurin, AIFD

Editor: Talmage McLaurin, AIFD

Authors: Shelley Urban, Kelsey Smith, Amy Bauer and David Coake

Art Directors: Linda Kunkle Park, Holly Cott

Copy Editors: David Coake, Shelley Urban and Cynthia McGowan

Photographers: John Collins and Stephen Smith

© 2013, Florists' Review Enterprises, Inc.

All Rights Reserved.

No part of this publication may be reproduced without
prior written permission from the publisher.

Christmas Classics was produced by Florists' Review Enterprises, Inc.,
Topeka, Kansas; www. floristsreview.com.

Printed in China

ISBN: 978-0-9854743-2-4

Florists' Review Enterprises is the leading magazine and book
publishing company for the U.S. floral industry. The company
is home to *Florists' Review* and *Super Floral Retailing* magazines
as well as to Florists' Review Bookstore, the industry's premier
marketplace for books and other educational materials.